MALALA YOUSAFZAI
Fighting for an Education

Peachtree

BY NATHAN SACKS

Published by The Child's World®
1980 Lookout Drive • Mankato, MN 56003-1705
800-599-READ • www.childsworld.com

Acknowledgments
The Child's World®: Mary Berendes, Publishing Director
Red Line Editorial: Design, editorial direction, and production
Photographs ©: Anthony Behar/Sipa USA/AP Images, cover, 1; Shahid Khan/
Shutterstock Images, 4; Facundo Arrizabalaga/EPA/Corbis, 6; Ishtiaq Mahsud/AP
Images, 8; Mohammad Sajjad/AP Images, 11; Anja Niedringhaus/AP Images, 12;
University Hospitals Birmingham/PA Wire/AP Images, 14; Eskinder Debebe/UN Photo/
AP Images, 16; Mary Altaffer/AP Images, 18; Heiko Junge/NTB Scanpix/AP Images, 20

ISBN 9781634074742

LCCN 2015946338

Printed in the United States of America
Mankato, MN
December, 2015
PA02286

ABOUT THE AUTHOR

Nathan Sacks is a writer and professional writing instructor from Ames, Iowa.
He currently lives in Minneapolis, Minnesota. He has written several other
books for children.

TABLE OF
CONTENTS

Chapter 1

Peaceful Beginnings 4

Chapter 2

Enter the Taliban 8

Chapter 3

Surviving an Assassin's Bullet 14

Chapter 4

Malala the Celebrity 18

Glossary 22
Source Notes 23
To Learn More 24
Index 24

Chapter 1

PEACEFUL BEGINNINGS

The northern part of Pakistan is full of green valleys and tall mountains. One of the most beautiful areas is the Swat District. It is located in northern Pakistan. The snow-capped Kush Mountains tower nearby. The green plains stretch across the land. In 1997, Malala Yousafzai was born there. Like the mountains and valleys of Pakistan, Malala became a symbol of the beauty and goodness of her country.

Before Malala became famous, she was just a regular girl. Before she knew celebrities like Angelina Jolie and Bono, she was just a girl who wanted to go to school. Her father, Ziauddin, ran the school that she attended. Malala adored her father. Because of him, Malala was interested in education from an early age. Promoting freedom and education for girls around the world would become her passion.

Malala's mother, Tor Pekai, is a **traditional Pashtun** Muslim mother. The Pashtun are a race of warriors who live in Afghanistan and Pakistan. Malala's family is Pashtun. Tor Pekai was very social. Friends and neighbors were always invited to their family home. Malala's mother could not read or write. She taught her daughter the traditions of Pakistani households. Malala was very close with her parents.

Growing up, Malala loved her faith. But she also enjoyed American pop culture. Once, Malala and her family visited the big city of Islamabad. There, Malala saw DVDs of American TV shows and movies that she wanted to buy. One of her favorites was *Ugly Betty*, a TV show about a young woman working for a fashion magazine. Malala also read the *Twilight* book series. She listened to music by Justin Bieber. Many traditional Muslims did not

▲ Malala Yousafzai dreamed of being a doctor when she grew up, but now she wants to be prime minister of Pakistan.

believe that women should read American books or watch TV. Some in the community warned Ziauddin that he was being too **permissive**. Some people thought Malala was not acting enough like a traditional Muslim.

Malala was lucky to attend school. In her country, more than 7 million children did not go to school. In Pakistan, girls could not attend schools with boys. There were fewer schools for girls. Many young girls never get an education.

Malala's school years were hard sometimes. Because her father ran the school, some people thought she was treated better than the other students. Some people thought she did not deserve her good grades. A few times, Malala had to submit papers to another school to prove she wasn't getting special treatment.

Meanwhile, the country of Pakistan was in trouble. From nearby Afghanistan, a Muslim terrorist group called the Taliban was approaching. They had a strict interpretation of the **Qur'an**, the Muslim holy book. They would kill anyone who disagreed with them. As the Taliban moved into cities in Pakistan, they killed people. They burned towns. Their followers were everywhere.

When Malala was born, the Swat Valley was free from Taliban rule. People still argued about Islamic law. But no one was killing anyone over these rules. That started to change when Malala was 10 years old. The Taliban began to grow in power. Soon, there was danger everywhere.

Chapter 2

ENTER THE TALIBAN

The Taliban were one of a few terrorist groups fighting American forces in Afghanistan. The United States invaded Afghanistan in 2002 after the September 11 terrorist attacks on the United States. The United States was successful in defeating the Taliban at first. But the Taliban had separate bases in Pakistan. In the Swat Valley, they could train. Then, they could strike back at their American enemies.

The Taliban began to slowly take over Swat in 2007. They started spreading messages of fear and violence. This helped them pursue **Sharia** law. Under this law, men had to have beards. All women needed to be veiled. Not everyone was happy with these rules. But the Swat government had little power. It did not fight back against the Taliban. Soon Taliban members were stopping people at security checkpoints. They were throwing people in jail for minor crimes. Then they started banning TV

WHO ARE THE TALIBAN?

The Taliban are a group of radical Sunni Muslims. Sunnis make up the largest branch of Islam, followed by the Shiites. Differences between Sunnis and Shiites have been the causes of many wars in the Islamic world. The Taliban was formed in the early 1990s in northern Pakistan. They are known for traditional practices, such as public executions and keeping women veiled. They also have very critical views of the West and America. They are known for banning TV, music, movies, and other forms of American culture.

and music. Malala's beautiful hometown had changed. It was becoming a dangerous and restricted place.

Malala and her family saw the Swat change. They were scared. One thing that the Taliban especially disliked was girls' access to education. In public, Malala's family had to be careful about what they said. At home, they still talked about TV, music, poetry, and science. Ziauddin told his daughter, "We must live a full life, if only in our hearts."[1]

Then, things got worse. Citizens hid or burned any music or books they owned that could get them into trouble with the Taliban. Malala and her family saw this. One night Malala asked her father, "Aba, will we have to burn our TV as well?"[2] Not long afterward, they hid their TV in the closet. Soon, the family had to flee town for a few days. A Taliban leader had threatened Ziauddin with death for speaking out against the Taliban.

Threats of violence kept many from speaking out. But they inspired Malala to act. In September 2008, at the age of 11, she went with her father to speak at a local press club. "How dare the Taliban take away my basic right to education!"[3] she cried. She talked about how she had to hide her textbooks under her clothes. The Taliban thought that any book that wasn't the Koran was dangerous.

▲ A building in Lahore, Pakistan, caught fire after a bomb from the Taliban exploded in May 2009.

Malala kept speaking out. In early 2009, she began blogging about her life for the BBC Urdu Web site, a branch of the British news organization that covered Indian and Pakistani news. The blog was called "Diary of a Pakistani Schoolgirl." At first, it was **anonymous**. Things were very dangerous now in northern

▲ **Before Malala and her school friends attended school in secret, they went to the Khushal school for girls.**

Pakistan. Policemen were found dead in the street. Hundreds of schools were closed or bombed. Malala had to be careful. But Malala caught the Taliban's attention. They found out that she was the blogger. Soon, the Taliban started sending very serious threats to Malala. They threatened her life.

October 9, 2012, was almost a day "like any other," according to Malala.[4] Malala and her friends had been going to school in secret. In the morning, she took a bus home after an exam. As they were passing a snack factory, the bus slowed down. A man with a mask and a gun walked onto the bus.

"Who is Malala?" he yelled.[5] The other students didn't respond, but looked at Malala. That was all the gunman needed to know his target. The man aimed his gun at her. Girls on the bus started to scream. Malala squeezed her friend's hand and closed her eyes. The gunman shot at her three times, hitting her once through the left eye. The bullet traveled down her body through her shoulder. Malala fell into the lap of her friend next to her. Blood was rushing from her head and ear. The remaining shots hit the two girls sitting by Malala. Malala blacked out. She never even heard the bullets.

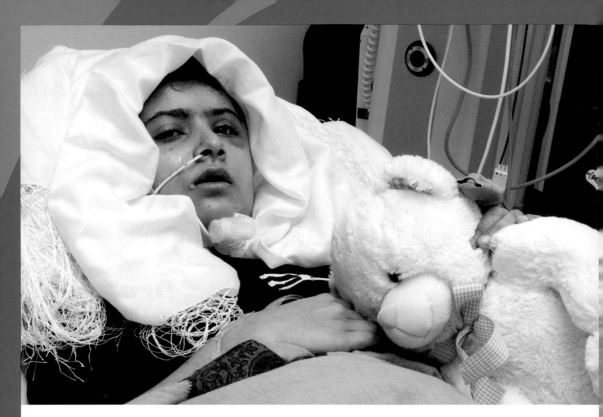

Chapter 3

SURVIVING AN ASSASSIN'S BULLET

Malala woke up alone in a hospital one week later. She had no idea what had happened. Her first thought was, *"Thank God I'm not dead."*[6]

She was no longer in Pakistan. She was now in a hospital in Birmingham, England. Malala's family was still back in Pakistan. Many doctors stood over her. Whirring, beeping machines surrounded her.

Because of the damage to her face, Malala could not speak at first. She had to trace letters with her hand to talk to people. The first thing she asked with her hands was *"Why have I no father?"*[7]

Malala was scared and in a lot of pain. Her head ached and she couldn't hear out of her left ear. Her jaw didn't move like it should. After five days of rest, Malala started to feel better. Eventually, she was able to talk again. But it would be six months before Malala's face would start to move like normal.

Malala's parents came to visit her in the hospital. Her father told her that only two people were arrested for her shooting. Both had nothing to do with the crime. A Pakistani minister pledged a $1 million reward for whoever could find the real shooter.

Many celebrities and journalists tried to visit Malala in the hospital. They were turned away so Malala could recover. But the story of Malala was spreading. People around the world were becoming interested.

It wasn't just celebrities and politicians who were paying attention to Malala. Things were changing in Pakistan, even

with Malala gone. Thousands of young people in the Swat region were inspired to campaign for the education rights of all Pakistani children.

In 2012, former British **prime minister**, Gordon Brown, declared November 10 to be a global day of action. It is also known as "Malala Day." On that day, he traveled to Pakistan to give the president of Pakistan a **petition**. The petition held more than one million signatures. It asked Pakistan President Zardari to "make education a reality for all Pakistani children."[8] That same year, Malala and her father founded the Malala Fund. This organization fights for the education rights of 62 million girls around the world. Brown called Malala "a brave, courageous, wonderful young woman." He said she can "show the world that good can come when you stand up for your **principles**."[9]

Malala later wrote, "The Taliban shot me to silence me—instead, the whole world is listening to my message now."[10]

◀ **Malala with the secretary general of the United Nations, Ban Ki-moon, at the UN headquarters in New York**

Chapter 4

MALALA THE CELEBRITY

The attempted assassination of Malala Yousafzai made her one of the most famous people in the world. Suddenly, she saw herself on the covers of magazines that she used to read in Islamabad. Angelina Jolie sent a message to her in the hospital. Selena Gomez tweeted about her. Madonna dedicated the song "Human Nature" to her. Beyoncé mentioned her on

Facebook. Malala was still a teenage girl at heart. To her, all this attention seemed like a very strange dream.

After Malala recovered, she gave speeches. She appeared on TV for interviews. She became a well-known speaker on education equality issues. One of the greatest moments of her life was when she spoke to the United Nations General Assembly in July 2013. Statesmen all over the world were stunned by her passionate speech. "One child, one teacher, one book, and one pen can change the world," she said as everyone cheered.[12] The audience gave her a standing ovation. Many newspapers reprinted her speech.

On October 10, 2014, Malala was in her morning chemistry class in Birmingham. Her teacher called her aside to give her some exciting news. Malala had won the Nobel Peace Prize. Malala knew she was being considered for the award, but she never thought she would win. She was shocked. Malala won the award along with Kailash Satyarthi, who is also an education activist. It was very unusual for a teenager even to be considered for this prize. At the age of 17, Malala was the youngest person ever to receive the prize.

▲ **Malala and Kailash Satyarthi held up their Nobel Peace Prizes for everyone to see.**

Two years after Malala was shot, she finally received justice. As of spring 2015, two men were arrested for their roles in the shooting of Malala. On April 30, 2015, those men were sentenced to life in prison.

Today, Malala is more loved than ever. She has inspired millions to make the world a better place. But for Malala, life is sometimes sad and lonely. She still lives in Birmingham, England. She is unable to go home to Pakistan for fear of her life. Things have changed in Pakistan, but there are still dangerous people who want to hurt her and her cause. Her parents live with her in

Birmingham. This is especially difficult for her traditional mother, who had so many friends in Swat that she cannot go back to. But Malala's mother was inspired by her daughter to learn how to read and write.

Malala dreams of the day when she can see the Swat District's beautiful valleys and mountains again. When she was little, Malala's grandmother would tell her, "No Pashtun leaves his land of his own sweet will. Either he leaves from poverty or for love."[13]

Malala Yousafzai didn't leave Pakistan because of poverty or love. She left because her life was in danger. But Malala dreams of a day when education is free and available to all, especially to young women. The day that world comes to be is the day she can return home to the land she loves most. For that reason and others, Malala keeps fighting.

NOBEL PEACE PRIZE

The Nobel Peace Prize is an award given by a Swedish organization, the Nobel Committee. Each year, the committee gives this award to the person who has done the most to champion the cause of peace in the world. Past winners include Theodore Roosevelt, Martin Luther King Jr., Nelson Mandela, and Barack Obama.

GLOSSARY

anonymous (a-NON-y-mus): Anonymous is an unknown author or unknown name. When Malala started writing her blog, it was anonymous.

Koran (kuh-RAN): The Koran is the main sacred book for Muslims. The Taliban didn't like any books that were not the Koran.

Pashtun (POSH-toon): The Pashtun are an ethnic group in southern Afghanistan and northwestern Pakistan. Malala's mother was Pashtun.

permissive (per-MIS-sive): Permissive is granting permission or allowing something. Malala's father was permissive when she wanted to watch American TV.

petition (pe-TISH-in): A petition is a written request or demand, often with signatures. Malala started a petition for the president of Pakistan to get every child in school.

prime minister (prahym min-UH-ster): A prime minister is the main leader in many countries. Gordon Brown was prime minister of the United Kingdom when he helped Malala make a change in Pakistan.

principles (PRIN-ci-puhls): Principles are rules or beliefs. Malala stood up for her principles against the Taliban, even though it meant putting herself in harm's way.

Sharia (shah-REE-ah): The Sharia laws are a set of strict religious laws that many Muslim countries follow. The Taliban enforced Sharia law in Pakistan.

traditional (truh-DISH-uh-nl): Traditional is when something is based on custom or earlier beliefs. Malala's mother had more traditional beliefs and was more religious.

SOURCE NOTES

1. Malala Yousafzai and Patricia McCormick. *I am Malala: How One Girl Stood Up for Education and Changed the World.* New York: Little, Brown and Company, 2014. Print. 46.

2. Ibid. 47.

3. Dhiya Kuriakose. "Malala Yousafzai: From Blogger to Nobel Peace Prize Nominee- Timeline." *The Guardian.* Guardian News and Media Limited, 9 Oct. 2013. Web. 12 May 2015.

4. Malala Yousafzai and Christina Lamb. *I am Malala: The Girl Who Stood Up for Education and Was Shot by the Taliban.* New York: Little, Brown and Company, 2013. Print. 3.

5. Steve Myall, "Malala Yousafzai Tells of the Moment She Was Shot in the Head by the Taliban." *Daily Mirror.* n.p., 13 Oct. 2013. Web. 12 May 2015.

6. McCormick. 133.

7. Ibid. 135.

8. Gordon Brown. "Stand With Malala on November 10th." *Huffington Post.* The HuffingtonPost.com, Inc., 22 Oct. 2012. Web. 6 Aug. 2015.

9. Abdul Hai Kakar. "Gordon Brown: Malala Proves One Person Can Make a Difference." *Radio Free Europe/Radio Liberty.* RFE/RL, Inc., 8 Oct. 2013. Web. 12 May 2015.

10. Inez Sarkodee-Adoo. "Malala Yousafzai: 'People are Listening to Me. But I Know That Might Change.'" *The Guardian.* Guardian News and Media Limited, 24 Aug. 2014. Web. 12 May 2015.

11. Malala Yousafzai. "Malala Yousafzai's Speech at the Youth Takeover of the United Nations." *A World at School.* n.p., n.d. Web. 12 May 2015.

12. Malala Yousafzai. "The Full Text: Malala Yousafzai Delivers Defiant Riposte to Taliban Militants with Speech to UN General Assembly." *The Independent.* independent.co.uk, 12 Jul. 2013. Web. 12 May 2015.

13. Lamb. 65.

TO LEARN MORE

Books

Abouraya, Karen Leggett and L.C. Wheatley. *Malala Yousafzai: Warrior With Words*. Great Neck, NY: StarWalk Kids Media, 2014.

Aretha, David. *Malala Yousafzai and the Girls of Pakistan*. Greensboro, NC: Morgan Reynolds Publishing, 2014.

Yousafzai, Malala with Patricia McCormick. *I am Malala: How One Girl Stood Up for Education and Changed the World*. New York: Little, Brown and Company, 2014.

Web Sites

Visit our Web site for links about Malala Yousafzai:

childsworld.com/links

Note to Parents, Teachers, and Librarians: We routinely verify our Web links to make sure they are safe and active sites. So encourage your readers to check them out!

INDEX

Afghanistan, 5, 7, 8

Birmingham, England, 14, 19, 20, 21

Brown, Gordon, 17

education, 5, 7, 10, 17, 19, 21

Ki-moon, Ban, 17

Koran, 7, 10

Malala Fund, 17

Muslim, 5, 6, 7, 9

Nobel Peace Prize, 19, 20, 21

Pakistan, 4, 5, 7, 8, 9, 11–12, 15, 17, 20, 21

Satyarthi, Kailash, 19, 20

Swat, 4, 7, 8, 9, 10, 17, 21

Taliban, 7, 8–11, 12–13

United Nations, 17, 19

Yousafzai, Tor Pekai, 5

Yousafzai, Ziauddin, 5, 6, 10